Dedicated to:

Sharon Leal Flood
who believes that volunteers and students
on placement cause awesome things to happen
and who always recognizes these individuals
personally in such an inclusive and meaningful way.

Sylvia Leal
who was a strong supporter of the volunteer
and student on placement programs and proudly
supported a project to increase the number of youth
volunteers in the after-school programs.

Copyright© 2020 by JiJi Talmas

All rights reserved. No part of this book may be reproduced in any form or by any electronic or mechanical means, including information storage and retrieval systems, without permission in writing from the publisher, except by reviewers, who may quote brief passages in a review. When pertinent © attibutions on derivatives to open source Creative Commons, Pixabay, Freepik, Vecteezy, CleanPNG, & other contributors providing Fair Use sources.

ISBN 978-1-7771579-1-3

Cataloging in Publication data block
1. Inspirational - Fiction 2. Adventure - Fiction

Written by JiJi Talmas

Cover and interior illustrations by José Gascón

Book design by José Gascón

Published by JiJi Talmas

The Author, JiJi Talmas is an Early Childhood Educator who is specialized
in working with children with great passion since 1995.
JiJi is a 2016/17 Award of Excellence recipient
and 2017/18 Kathleen Stroud Award recipient.

My Classroom is the best this year
For we have a special volunteer

SHE IS AWESOME, SHE IS FUN AND REAL SWEET

USING OUR IMAGINATION
TAKING US TO AN ADVENTURE
THAT SEEMS SO REAL

When I write my name, she helps me to keep it neat

In block play, we build bridges, houses, and streets

A GREAT BIG TOWER...
AS TALL AS OUR VOLUNTEER!

THIS SECTION IS DEDICATED TO YOUR VOLUNTEER.
YOU COULD DRAW A PICTURE ADD A PHOTO,

OR JUST WRITE A NOTE OF APPRECIATION.

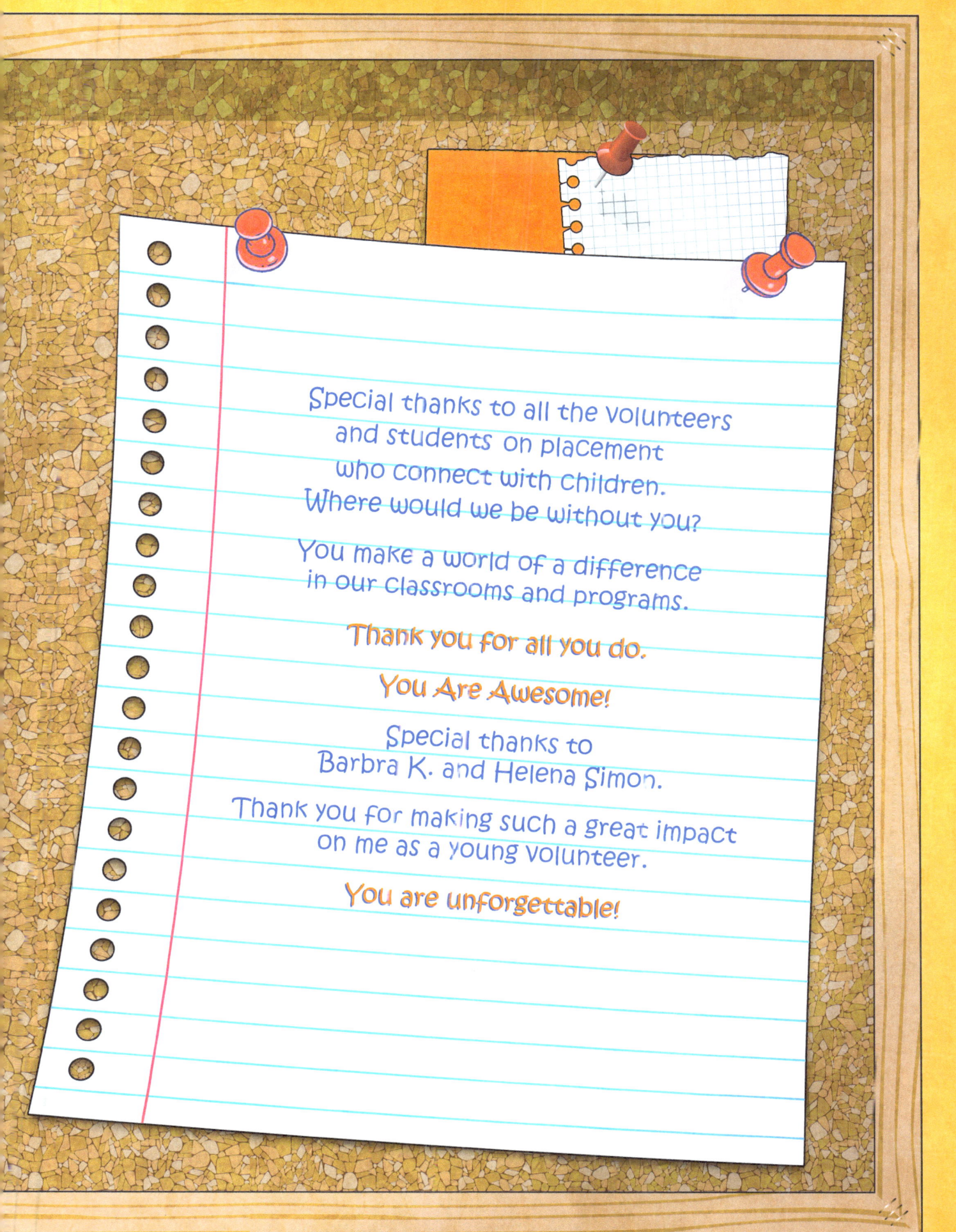

Special thanks to all the volunteers and students on placement who connect with children. Where would we be without you?

You make a world of a difference in our classrooms and programs.

Thank you for all you do.

You Are Awesome!

Special thanks to Barbra K. and Helena Simon.

Thank you for making such a great impact on me as a young volunteer.

You are unforgettable!

www.ingramcontent.com/pod-product-compliance
Lightning Source LLC
Chambersburg PA
CBHW042256100526
44589CB00002B/42